Polish Cooking

TEXT: RAFAŁ JABŁOŃSKI
PHOTOGRAPHY: JOLANTA
AND RAFAŁ JABŁOŃSKI

FESTINA

Table of contents

CONTENTS

Introduction

Contemporary Polish cuisine derives from centuries of culinary tradition, influenced by many factors.

One of these was location and resulting from this the range of resources available at this latitude. Since time immemorial large forests have provided Poles with mushrooms, berries, raspberries and honey, and fertile agricultural lands crops, such as corn, peas, grits, meat and milk. These and other available resources were processed in the kitchen in various ways, and the old Poles' palate was decisive for the choice of available range of favourite dishes. Therefore, medieval cuisine was full of meat, fish and grits, which were then added to almost every dish. Soups, called 'polewki' (pottages), were not disliked. The most popular of them were 'barszcz' (beetroot soup), 'żur' (sour soup), 'czernina' (duck blood soup) and 'flaki' (tripe). No hunt could have been made without 'bigos' (sauerkraut stew), with frequently added meat from the hunters' prey. Meals at noble manors consisted of the so-called Prendium, or early lunch, and Coena – early dinner.

The second factor was religion, which already in pagan times gave dishes ritual meaning. 'Pierogi' (dumplings), resembling the sun with its rays, are associated with a solar cult that was practiced in the areas of today's Poland, for

Ciechanowiec. Open air museum.

example at Ślęża Mountain. An egg, as the origin of new life, became a symbol of rebirth and the beginning of the world, and a poppy, with a multitude of seeds, was regarded as a symbol of fertility.

Wzgiezłów. Open air museum.

In the Christian times part of pagan beliefs was adopted into the new faith practices. E.g. 'pierogi', (dumplings), were originally served only during the holidays, and egg, as a symbol of the resurrection of Christ, was served at Easter time.

Biłgoraj. Heritage Park Sitarska.

Many fasts, restrictively respected, were treated as a spiritual preparation for the church holidays, celebrated sumptuously, with a richly laid table. Thus the tradition of typical holiday dishes emerged, which were a particularly expected luxury that not everyone could afford to in their everyday life.

The third factor was the influence of different

cooking methods and the use of new resources, which arrived in Poland from other, sometimes very distant, countries. In the Middle Ages numerous contacts with the Orient resulted in availability of various spices imported from the Far East, mainly from India. It was Queen Jadwiga in the fourteenth century who introduced to the Polish cuisine a fashion for the rich use of pepper, nutmeg, saffron, cloves, etc. Due to the high prices of the eastern spices they were luxury goods, but at the same time often used, increasing the social status of the host who was giving a feast. For foreign visitors, especially the French, the food seemed too spicy. On the other hand, from the Orient also came to us all the sweets, such as sweetmeats: figs, raisins, almonds, dried fruits and sugar.

The wife of King Sigismund the Old, Bona Sforza, living in the early sixteenth century, was born in a wealthy family of the dukes of Milan. Moving to Cracow she took with her Italian chefs who introduced Italian cuisine to Polish cooking. Fat, meat dishes were enriched with vegetables, such as broccoli, celery, parsley, leek, cabbage, lettuce and tomatoes, which were not known in Polish cuisine, and it was necessary to import them directly from Italy.

During the reign of King John III Sobieski in Polish cuisine appeared potatoes. Seedlings imported by King from Vienna, which he defended against the Turks, were a gift for Queen Marysieńka. Initially they were adopted solely in aristocratic cooking. Commonly they were considered harmful to health and used only as a fodder for pigs. During the reign of King Augustus III (1736-1763), many German settlers,

Kolbuszowa. Heritage museum.

Biłgoraj. Sieve Farm.

who planted potatoes, contributed to the popularization of this dish.

In 1683 appeared the first cookery book 'Com-

Lednogra. Open air museum.>

pendium Ferculorum or Collection of the Dishes' written by Stanisław Czerniecki, which was the quintessence of baroque Polish cuisine. Still there was a trend for greasy food, seasoned with

Guciów. Guciów family Farm.

spicy or sour herbs, which were combined with the 'sweets'. Viscid, spicy sauces were used for stewing the dishes. Baroque decorativeness often dominated over the taste.

The end of the seventeenth century, and especially the times of King Stanislaus Augustus Poniatowski and his famous Thursday dinners, brought fashion for culinary French trends. The King's chef, Paulo Tremo, whose culinary handwritten notes have survived to our time, introduced to the royal table (and through it to the tables of the nobility) a fashion for sophisticated dishes with a delicate flavour. It is true that he tried to make a synthesis of the tastes of the two mutually exclusive worlds, but a change inevitably followed. Traditional old Polish cuisine with hot, sour, peppery and saffron flavours went down in history. Released in 1786 'An Excellent Cook' by Wojciech Wielądek, is a quite accurate, although brief, translation of the popular in France in the late eighteenth century 'Cuisinier Bourgeoise' which did not include even one traditional Polish recipe. From France also came the fashion for three meals instead of two. Breakfast, lunch with soup and a second dish, and dinner have maintained to our times.

The end of the eighteenth century brought the tragedy of the partition of Poland, by the three invaders: Prussia, Austria and Russia. 123 years of annexation of the country, divided into three

Ciechanowiec. Living room of a mansion in the Heritage Museum.

arts, contributed substantially to the country's culinary tastes. Its every part, included in the foreign state, automatically accepted cultural patterns of the invaders. Thus, culinary differ-

ences were born, which also continued to our times, although in many cases mainly in relation to names. One example could be potatoes, called 'pyry' in Greater Poland, 'kartofle' in Silesia,

365 OBIADÓW

ZA 5 ZŁOTYCH,

AUTORKĘ JEDYNYCH PRAKTYCZNYCH
PRZEPISÓW.

120 obiadów postnych bez ryb.

Nakładem Autorki.

WARSZAWA.

1871.

*'365 Dinners for Five Zloties' of 1858 by Lucyna
Ćwierczakiewiczowa.*

were taken from eighteenth-century gentry calendars. They contained dishes characteristic for the Polish gentry from the end of the Nobility Commonwealth times.

The People's Republic of Poland period was of course, the time of Polish cuisine collapse but since 1992, along with political changes, there came a rapid return to traditional Polish and regional cuisine. Old recipes, buried deep in both the memory of older people and old dressers were dug out. Traditional home cooking, by 'grandmother's recipe' came back into fashion again.

This book presents the dishes cooked by such recipes.

'grule' in the mountains, and 'bulwy' (bulbs) in Kashubia. Potatoes in the nineteenth century became the main dish, as was formerly grits. The invaders, prepared for predatory exploitation of the former Polish territories, caused the impoverishment of the Polish society, which was particularly noticeable in the rural areas. Potatoes, as a nutritious and easy to prepare dish, met the dietary requirements.

During the time of the partition, there were also trends toward maintaining Polish culinary tradition. An example could be the cookbook '365 Dinners for Five Zloties' of 1858 by Lucyna Ćwierczakiewiczowa, the recipes of which

Nieborów. Palace. Venetian Room. >

TATAR BEEFSTEAK
(BEFSZTYK TATARSKI)

Originally it was a dish made from the horse meat by the Tatar tribes inhabiting the steppes of Asia and settling on Polish territory since the fourteenth century. At the same time beef tartar was known in Western Europe and recommended as a dish for people in need of strengthening the body.

Preparation

Chop well washed fillets, scrape or mince to small pieces in a machine. Lay a circular portion on a plate and create a hollow in the middle. Place the egg yolks in it. Dice onions, cucumbers and mushrooms and place next to the meat on the plate. Before eating, mix all the ingredients and season with salt, pepper, maggi and mustard to taste, and add olive oil.

INGREDIENTS:

- 500 grams of beef sirloin - 2 onions - 2 pickled cucumbers - 4 egg yolks - 4 pickled mushrooms - 1 teaspoon of olive oil - mustard - maggi - salt - ground pepper

*B*IGOS
(SAUERKRAUT STEW)

The name 'bigos' comes from Latin and means two flavours, or from the German 'beigossen' – which means 'to pour'. In medieval Poland, the word was used to describe chopping. In the gentry manors 'bigos' was often served during hunts. It was a popular custom to close the pot with a lid sealed with dough. Ready-to-eat food was signalised by a loud 'firing' of the cover, due to pressure that emerged during the cooking.

Preparation of sauerkraut stew

Chop fresh cabbage and sauerkraut and pour over boiling water. Dice all kinds of meat and fry in a pan. Chop the onion and soaked mushrooms. Fry chopped onion until its golden brown. All these ingredients add to the cabbage. Season to taste with salt and pepper and put a few bay leaves and allspice. Pour in the wine. Mix the whole and cook for about an hour. Reheat for the next three days. In the winter, at night, you can put it outside to freeze.

INGREDIENTS:

- 400 grams of sauerkraut - 400 grams of cabbage - 200 grams of boneless pork - 200 grams of veal - 250 grams of sausage - 100 g grams smoked bacon - 50 grams of pork fat - 2 onions - 10 grams of dried mushrooms - salt - ground pepper - sugar - a few prunes - all spice - bay leaf - 1 glass of dry wine

PIG'S TROTTERS IN ASPIC

(GALARETKA Z NÓŻEK)

Preparation

Cleaned and singe over the fire the pig's trotters. Cook with a pork knuckle in a pot filled with water for 1 hour. Add onion, salt, pepper and cleaned greens, and cook everything until soft. At the end of cooking add the garlic. Peel the trotters and pork meat and dice. Pour a little of the strained broth on the bottom of the bowls and let it cool down. On this layer put the meat and pour the broth to cover the meat. You can add chopped carrots to the bowl. Cool down to solidify and serve with vinegar or horseradish.

INGREDIENTS:
- 4 pig's trotters
- 1 knuckle of pork
- 250 grams of soup greens
- 2 onions
- 12 grains of pepper
- allspice - bay leaves
- 1 clove of garlic - salt
- ground pepper

CARP IN ASPIC
(KARP W GALARECIE)

Preparation

Dip the carp in boiling water for a while and scrape, cut off the head and fins, cut into slices. Cut out the gills for the dish was not bitter. Lightly salt the fish and put in the fridge. Put into the pot rinsed and scraped greens, head and fins of carp, crushed garlic, chopped onion and spices. Pour cold water, covering the contents of the pot. Cook until tender. Strain the contents, except the carrots. Place the slices of the carp in the broth, add salt and pepper and cook until tender. Spread gelatine in 150 ml of cold water. At the end of the cooking pour the gelatine into the pot and stir well. Cool the contents of the pot, but not to a state of coagulation. Take out the carrot and cut it into strips. Take out the carp and arrange on a platter. Put the carrot next to it and pour the thickening broth into the whole.

INGREDIENTS:

- 1 carp - 2 onions - bunch of soup greens
- juice from 0.5 of lemon - allspice
- bay leaf - thyme - 1 tablespoon of gelatine
- salt - ground pepper

VEGETABLE SALAD

Preparation

Peel the carrots, celery and parsley and drop into the pot. Add water and cook until soft. Cook potatoes in their skins until tender. Boil eggs hard. Peel the potatoes and apples. Dice all the ingredients. Pour in the canned peas. Add salt, pepper, mustard and mayonnaise, paying particular attention to its quality. Stir everything together and set aside in a cool place.

INGREDIENTS:
- 4 carrots
- 2 parsley (root)
- 3 potatoes
- 1 small celery
- 6 pickled cucumbers
- 5 hard-boiled eggs
- 1 can of peas
- salt
- ground pepper
- 1 tablespoon of mustard
- 6 tablespoons of mayonnaise
- 2 apples

HERRINGS IN CREAM
(ŚLEDZ W ŚMIETANIE)

Preparation

Soak the herrings in water for about 1 hour and cut into strips. Apple and cucumber grate on a coarse grater. Dice the onion. All the ingredients add to the herrings. Add the cream, mix carefully and store in the refrigerator for at least 1 hour.

INGREDIENTS:

- 4-5 slices of herring in oil (matias)
- 1 apple
- 4 pickled cucumbers
- 1 onion
- 30 grams of sour cream (18% of fat)

Soups

BARSZCZ
(BEETROOT SOUP)

Soup of this name derives from a herb common in Poland called 'barszcz', soured with acid from rye flour. Not until later did it begin to be made with beetroot. The first mention of beetroot soup comes from King Ladislaus Jagiello times, i.e. the fifteenth century.

Pickling of red beetroot soup

Peel beetroot, cut into slices and put into a jar or clay pot. Pour salted water in a ratio of 1 tablespoon per 1 litre of water, so that it covers the beetroot. Add the garlic and let it stand for two weeks in a warm place. Strain the juice into a glass bottle and store in a cool place.

Preparation of the soup

Pour water onto the meat, clean and cut into quarters the beetroot, clean the vegetables, soak the mushrooms and peel and cut onions. Place over a low heat. Cook until tender. Strain the broth, add beetroot acid and season with garlic, pepper and salt. Beetroot soup can also be cooked from stock of broth from different kinds of meat.

Preparation of ravioli

Prepare the dough as for 'pierogi' (dumplings). Mince the meat from the broth, add onion, chopped up small and browned in a frying pan, together with chopped and previously soaked mushrooms. Season with spices to taste. Wrap the stuffing in pre-cut ravioli.

INGREDIENTS:

Pickling of Barszcz:
- *1.5 kilograms of beetroot*
- *a piece of rye bread*
- *salt*
- *garlic*

Beetroot soup:
- *1.5 litres of water*
- *500 grams of beetroot*
- *300 grams of meat on the bone*
- *200 grams of greens*
- *10 grams of dried mushrooms*
- *50 grams of onion*
- *0.5 liter of beetroot juice*
- *1 bay leaf*
- *1 clove of garlic*
- *ground pepper*
- *salt*
- *sugar*

Ravioli:
- *150 grams of flour*
- *1 egg*
- *1 onion*

CHŁODNIK
(COLD SOUP)

Soup prepared cold. Its origin comes from Lithuania, as indicates the often used nickname 'Lithuanian'. First mentioned in the literature in the national epic 'Pan Tadeusz' of 1811, by Adam Mickiewicz.

Preparation

Dice all the ingredients, throw into the curdled milk and stir. Add the beetroot juice. Season with salt and pepper. Put into the refrigerator for several hours.

You can also add chopped and pre-baked pieces of meat: poultry or veal.

Cold soup with soft-boiled, diced fresh beetroots is called Lithuanian.

INGREDIENTS:

- 1 litre of curdled milk
- beetroot juice
- two green cucumbers
- 6 radishes - dill - chives
- salt - ground pepper
- sugar - 3 eggs
- 2 tomatoes

22

CZERNINA
(DUCK BLOOD SOUP)

Traditional Polish soup, so called 'black pottage', served in the old days to a cavalier as a refusal of maiden's hand, that he had asked for. The name derives from a dialect term, from Kuyavia, for 'black pottage' – 'Czornina'. In Mazovia it is known as 'Gray Pottage'.

Preparation

Mix the blood with vinegar, so as not to curdle. Toss into the pot with duck, giblets, cleansed greens and spices. Pour in cold water and cook until tender. Strain the broth, pour the blood in. Add cloves, a spoonful of sugar and boil. Meat and giblets are then cut into pieces and dropped into the soup.

Duck blood soup can be served with noodles.

INGREDIENTS:

- 0.5 of a duck
- 1 glass of duck blood
- 0.5 of a glass of vinegar
- duck giblets (maw, liver, heart, feet)
- 1 onion - bay leaves - allspice
- 2 cloves - 1 tablespoon of sugar - pasta

RIPE
(FLAKI)

This dish was known in Poland since the fifteenth century. It was popular during the reign of King Ladislaus Jagiello.

Preparation

Carefully clean the tripe and wash two times, put into a pot of salted water and boil. Cook, changing the water with new boiling water every 15 minutes. Repeat the change three times. Cook tripe over low heat until completely tender. Strain the tripe. Wash the meat and together with peeled greens and onion put into a pot of water. Add the bay leaf, marjoram, allspice, ginger, pepper, and salt and simmer for 1 hour. Add the tripe to the broth, season with spices and add a fried, chopped small onion.

INGREDIENTS:

- 1 kilogram of beef tripe
- 0.5 kilogram of chicken or beef meat on the bone - soup greens - ground pepper - salt
- marjoram - nutmeg - allspice - ground sweet pepper - bay leaf - ginger

PEA SOUP
WITH SMOKED BACON

Preparation

Soak the peas overnight in cold, previously boiled water. Cook the peas the next day in the same water until almost soft. Cook without lid as the peas can boil over. Dice the potatoes and carrots. Together with shredded garlic and ribs toss into the pot with water and cook until soft. Dice the sausage and onion and fry in a pan. Add all the ingredients to the peas. Season to taste with spices.

INGREDIENTS:

- *300 grams of whole peas*
- *3 potatoes*
- *2 carrots*
- *1-2 cloves of garlic*
- *150 grams of smoked ribs*
- *150 grams of fine sausages*
- *1 onion*
- *marjoram*
- *salt*
- *ground pepper*

APUŚNIAK
(SAUERKRAUT SOUP)

Preparation

Dice the ribs, add the greens, allspice, pepper and bay leaf and cook. When cooked, take out the greens. Shred the sauerkraut and cook in a separate pot in a larger amount of water. Dice bacon and onions and fry in a pan. Cook the diced and peeled potatoes. Add the ribs with a broth, bacon, onions and potatoes to the sauerkraut. Season to taste and cook for several minutes.

Another version of the sauerkraut soup is 'Kwaśnica', served in the Polish mountains. The tradition derives its origin from the Beskidy Mountains, where it was traditionally served at a formal boar hunt.

INGREDIENTS:

- 500 grams of sauerkraut - 250 grams of smoked ribs - 200 grams smoked bacon - potatoes - 1 onion - oil or lard - soup greens - salt - ground pepper - bay leaf - allspice

*B*ARLEY SOUP
(KRUPNIK)

Preparation

Put greens, ribs, bay leaf, allspice, and mushrooms into a pot of water. Singe the onions over the gas fire. Pour water into a pot, put the onion, add salt and pepper and boil. After boiling, pour the pearl barley, stirring gently. Simmer for about 40 minutes, occasionally stirring. Be careful and keep the pearl barley from sticking to the bottom of the pot and burning. Take out the meat, dice and put it back. Remove onions and greens.

INGREDIENTS:

- *300 grams of ribs*
- *soup greens - 1 onion*
- *cabbage - 2 potatoes*
- *3 tablespoons of butter*
- *bay leaf - 3 allspices*
- *100 grams of pearl barley*
- *mushrooms - salt*
- *ground pepper - allspice - bay leaf*

ROYAL BROTH
(ROSÓŁ KRÓLEWSKI)

A traditional soup that came about in old times as a result of prolonged cooking of meat. This resulted from the need for desalination of meat stored in brine and salted and then dried. The name 'Rosół' originates from desalination.

Preparation

Rinse the meat and put into a pot. Pour cold water and bring to boil over low heat. This method makes the most of the meat components which go into the broth. After 15 minutes of slow cooking remove so called 'dross' from the top. Put in peeled vegetables, spices and onion, singed over a gas fire. Simmer the broth for 4 hours, thereby obtaining purity of the soup. When cooked, strain all the ingredients.

Broth is served with pre-cooked pasta, preferably home-made. Pour chopped parsley to the whole. You can leave pieces of cooked carrot in the broth. Add a little sugar.

Preparation of pasta

Sift the flour. Add eggs, salt, and knead the dough for about 5-10 minutes. Set it aside for 30 minutes, covered with a cloth – thus it loses its flexibility. Roll out the dough as thinly as possible and let it dry. Cut into strips of the required width. Cook pasta in salted water with olive oil.

INGREDIENTS:

Broth:
- *500 grams of beef*
- *0.25 of hen*
- *150 grams of veal - soup greens*
- *1 onion*
- *1 tablespoon of butter*
- *salt - ground pepper*
- *sugar*

Pasta:
- *2 glasses of wheat flour*
- *2 eggs - 4 egg yolks*

MUSH-ROOM SOUP
WITH NOODLES

A traditional soup served on Christmas Eve. For the first time it appeared in the literature in the cookery book by Lucyna Ćwierczakiewiczowa '365 Dinners' in 1860.

Preparation

Wash the mushrooms carefully, cover with cold water for 2 hours. Finely shred and throw into the broth. Then add chopped up small and fried onions and cook the whole until tender. Washed and diced greens are cooked separately. Greens with a broth are poured onto the mushrooms. Season with salt and pepper.

Serve with noodles and a tablespoon of cream.

INGREDIENTS:

Mushroom Soup:
- soup greens - 5 medium potatoes - 500 grams of fresh mushrooms - 1 onion - 150 ml of cream - litres of water - 3 tablespoons of oil - salt - ground pepper - bay leaf - allspice

*N*OTHING'
SOUP
(ZUPA NIC)

Preparation

Boil the milk with grated vanilla beans. Carefully separate the whites of the eggs from the yolks.
Stiffly whip the white with sugar and put with
a table spoon on the milk. Cook on both sides for
2 minutes. Put the prepared dumplings on a plate.
Stir the egg yolks with sugar. Add slowly chilled
milk, still stirring. Stir until the mixture gets thick-
er. Add pre-soaked raisins and chopped up small
almonds. Pour the milk onto the dumplings.

INGREDIENTS:

- *1.25 litres of milk*
- *2 eggs*
- *vanilla bean*
- *100 grams of caster sugar*
- *100 grams of raisins*
- *100 grams of almonds*

ꞆOMATO SOUP
(ZUPA POMIDOROWA)

Preparation

Wash the meat and cover with water in a pot. Add the greens, pepper, salt, bay leaf, allspice and cook for about 1 hour. Strain the broth and mix with tomato juice. Cook for about 15 minutes. Put the pasta on a plate and pour in the tomato soup. Add basil and a teaspoon of cream. It's common to leave the carrot pieces in the soup.

INGREDIENTS:

- *250 grams of meat on the bone (chicken or veal)*
- *soup greens*
- *grated tomatoes or tomato juice*
- *salt*
- *ground pepper*
- *allspice*
- *bay leaf*
- *basil*

ŻUR
(SOUR SOUP)

The name 'żur' comes from Old German word 'sur', today's 'sauer' which means 'sour' and became popular in Poland around the fifteenth century. Originally, the dish was known primarily in Silesia, hence often used name 'Silesian sour soup'.

Pickling of sour soup

To a clay pot or glass jar pour the flour with enough hot water to get the consistency of batter. Add the bay leaf, allspice and garlic. After cooling down, add water and onion and crumbled bread or yeast. Mix the whole carefully. Cover with a cloth and let it stand in warm place for three or more days, depending on the storage temperature.

Preparation of soup

Peel vegetables, cut into large pieces, add the allspice, and cook for about 30 minutes. Peel the onion and dice along with the bacon. Fry in a pan. Peel the potatoes, cut into large cubes and cook. Remove vegetables from the broth and replace them with potatoes and bacon. Cook for 10 minutes. Pour the sourdough and season with salt, pepper and marjoram.

Sour soup can be served with whole or sliced sausage and with freshly hard-boiled egg.

INGREDIENTS:

Pickling of 'żur':
- 1 glass of rye flour
- a few cloves of garlic
- 1 onion - bay leaf
- a few grains of allspice
- half of a slice of wholemeal bread with the crust or 10 g of yeast
- 4 cups of cold, previously boiled water

Sour soup:
- 500 ml of sourdough for sour soup
- a bunch of soup greens
- 500 grams of white sausage
- 100 grams of smoked bacon
- salt - ground pepper
- marjoram - allspice - bay leaf

Veal

VEAL IN VEGETABLES
(CIELĘCINA W WARZYWACH)

Preparation

Wash the meat, rub in with salt, garlic, marjoram, grease with olive oil and set aside in a cool place for several hours. Cut the veal into strips, fry in a pan and throw into a pot of boiling water, so that it covers half of the meat. Wash the greens, scrape and grate on a coarse grater. Brown chopped mushrooms and onion and, together with dried mushrooms, add to the meat. Add spices and simmer until meat is tender. At the end of cooking, add a tablespoon of butter.

INGREDIENTS:

- 500 grams of boneless veal
- large soup greens
- 100 grams of mushrooms
- olive oil - dried mushrooms
- marjoram - allspice
- bay leaf - 1 tablespoon of butter
- salt - ground pepper

SCALOPES
(ESKALOPKI)

Preparation

Wash the meat, cut into slices and pestle. Add salt and pepper. Coat with flour and fry in hot butter for 3 minutes on each side. Arrange the meat in a casserole, sprinkle with grated cheese, sliced ham and parsley. Pour the broth into the butter, mix and add to the meat. Put in the oven preheated to 220°C and roast for 20 minutes.

INGREDIENTS:

- 500 grams of veal
- 150 grams of Parmesan cheese
- 150 grams of ham
- 2 tablespoons of chopped parsley
- 200 grams flour
- 60 grams of butter
- 5 tablespoons of broth
- salt
- ground pepper

$\mathcal{V}$EAL CUTLET
(SZNYCEL CIELĘCY)

Preparation

Wash the meat, remove the membranes, cut into portions across the fibres and pestle the meat cutlets. Sprinkle with spices and strew with flour scattered egg and bread crumbs. Fry on both sides until golden brown.

On top of the cutlet you can put a fried egg or cheese or mushrooms.

INGREDIENTS:

- 150 grams of boneless veal
- fat
- bread crumbs
- 20 grams flour
- 1 egg
- salt
- ground pepper

VEAL TONGUES
IN HORSERADISH SAUCE

Preparation

Put the entire ingredients into boiled water and cool down the marinade. Take the tongues and set aside in a cool place for 24 hours. Remove the tongues, strain and cook in vegetable broth until tender. When the tongues are still warm remove the skin and cut into centimetre-wide slices. To 1 litre of broth from the cooking of the tongues add horseradish and cream and cook for 10 minutes. When the sauce becomes thick add the yolk of eggs and cook for 1 minute. Add chopped parsley, lemon juice, sugar, salt and pepper. Pour the sauce into tongues.

INGREDIENTS:

- 0,5 kilogram of veal tongues - 1 litre of vegetable broth
Marinade:
- 2 tablespoons of salt - allspice - pepper - bay leaf - 0.5 of garlic bulb - 250 ml of water - 1 tablespoon of oil
Horseradish Sauce:
- 100 grams of grated horseradish - 1 litre of broth from cooking of tongues - 100 ml of cream - 2 egg yolks - parsley - salt - ground pepper - sugar - juice of 1 lemon

Beef

PIECE OF MEAT
IN HORSERADISH SAUCE

Preparation

Wash the meat and, together with cut into large pieces greens, put into a pot of boiling water. Add the bay leaf, pepper, allspice, marjoram and salt. Simmer until the meat is almost tender. When cooked, strain the meat and cool down 0.5 l of broth. Melt butter in a frying pan, sprinkle with flour and fry lightly. Mix with the broth, milk and egg yolks. Cook until the sauce thickens. Add finely grated horseradish and season with salt and pepper.

INGREDIENTS:

Meat:
- 0,5 kilogram of beef - 2 onions - 1 bunch of soup greens - allspice - 2 bay leaves - marjoram - salt - ground pepper
Horseradish Sauce:
- 10 grams of butter - 15 grams of flour
- 250 ml of milk - 2 egg yolks
- 100 grams of horseradish

WRAPPED LOBES
(ZRAZY ZAWIJANE)

A dish typical for Polish gentry and hunting cuisine. The name derives from the Old Polish word 'Zrazanie' meaning cutting off pieces of meat from the whole.

Preparation

Wash the meat and cut into slices across the fibres. Pestle the chops on both sides. Cucumbers, mushrooms and smoked bacon cut into chops-long strips. Salt and pepper the slices of meat, spread the mustard on them and place with bacon, cucumber and mushrooms. Wrap the meat with additives in a roll and fasten with a cotton thread or toothpick so it will not come apart. Fry lobes from both sides on low heat. Chop up small the onion. Boil water in a pot and put the meat and onion, bay leaves, dried mushrooms and other seasonings. Cook until tender. During the cooking, add a tablespoon of sugar and balsamic vinegar.

Serve the lobes with buckwheat porridge.

INGREDIENTS:

- 500 grams of boneless beef - 100 grams of smoked bacon or pork fat - 2 tablespoons of spicy mustard - dried mushrooms - 2 pickled cucumbers - 2 onions - marjoram - bay leaf - salt - ground pepper

Pork

ROASTED PORK KNUCKLE
(GOLONKA PIECZONA)

The dish originates from Germany. Adapted in the Polish territory throughout Greater Poland which in the years 1772 - 1918 was under Prussian annexation.

Preparation of marinade

To 1 litre of boiled water put all the spices. Cool down the broth. Put the pork knuckle so that it was fully covered with marinade. Place the lid and press with something heavy. Set aside in a cool place for 3-4 days. Shift the knuckle several times. Take the knuckle out from the marinade and put into cold water for as many hours as many days it stayed in the marinade. Change water several times.

Preparation of pork knuckle

Knuckle rub in with garlic, olive oil, salt, pepper and sweet pepper and fry on all sides. Place in the casserole with a little water. Roast in the oven for 2 hours. Uncover the lid and roast for another 30 minutes.

INGREDIENTS:

Broth:
- 1 litre of boiled water - 100 grams of salt - garlic
- allspice - marjoram - ground pepper - bay leaf
Pork knuckle:
- knuckle of pork - ground sweet pepper - salt
- ground pepper - garlic

STUFFED CABBAGE

(GOŁĄBKI)

A dish originating from the Eastern Borderlands, the region of Terespol. Originally, it was a Christmas Eve dish, made from buckwheat porridge and potatoes. In the course of time, with addition of meat, it has become a dinner dish.

Preparation

Cut down the cabbage-stump, put the cabbage into boiling water and cook for several minutes. Remove the leaves from the top one by one. If the next leaves are too hard cook the cabbage again. Remove all the leaves. Cut off and throw away the hard parts of the leaves or pestle them. Rinse the rice and cook in salted water. Set it aside, covered, in a warm place. Mince the meat, add the egg, pepper, salt, cayenne pepper, basil and fried, finely chopped onion. Mix all of it with cooled rice. On the cabbage leaf lay a small portion of meat with rice. Wrap the leaf tightly. At the bottom of the pot with water, put in the cabbage leaves, add salt, pepper, bay leaves and water. Place the stuffed cabbage and add the tomato puree. Cook for 2 hours. Set aside until the next day and cook for 15 minutes.

INGREDIENTS:

- cabbage head - 250 grams of minced pork
- 250 grams of beef - rice - egg - 1 onion
- a can of tomato puree - cayenne pepper
- basil - salt - ground pepper

45

PORK NECK
(KARKÓWKA)

Preparation

Wash the meat, rub with olive oil, garlic (you can make holes in the meat with a finger and put in the pieces of garlic), add salt, pepper, marjoram and put in cold place for a few hours. Slice the meat. Heat a large frying pan with oil, put the meat, add salt, pepper, diced peppers, onion, garlic and mushrooms. Add a can of corn with dressing, a jar of strained canned peppers, sliced leek and a lot of ketchup or tomato puree. Fry all together. Place in a casserole and roast for about 1.5 hours.

INGREDIENTS:

- *500 grams of pork neck*
- *1 red pepper*
- *1 yellow pepper*
- *1 large onion*
- *1 clove of garlic*
- *1 can of canned pepper*
- *1 can of corn*
- *1 leek*
- *tomato puree*
- *salt - ground pepper*

MEAT RISSOLES

WITH BEETROOTS

Preparation of chops

Wash meat, grind, add egg, pepper, salt, and finely chop. Fry the onions and soak the bread rolls. Mix and add 25 ml of cold, sparkling water. Shape the round meat balls. If your hands are sticky wet them in cold water. Coat the meat rissole in breadcrumbs and fry in hot oil.

To meat pulp, you can add chopped dill, and inside yellow cheese.

Preparation of beetroot

Boil the beets, peel the skin and grate. Add a little lemon, salt, pepper and a tablespoon of butter. To the beetroots you can add grated apple.

INGREDIENTS:

Chops:
- 500 grams of pork - 1 large onion
- 1 bread roll - 100 grams breadcrumbs
- 1 egg - Salt - Ground pepper
Beetroots:
- 500 grams of beetroots - Lemon
- Butter - Salt - Pepper

PORK CHOPS
WITH FRIED CABBAGE

In the Renaissance, in Italy, the food was covered with thin gold leafs. Bread-crumbing of meat originated as a cheaper substitute version of the exclusive decoration. This dish has been known in Poland since the nineteenth century. It appeared for the first time in Lucyna Ćwierczakiewiczowa's cookbook „365 Dinners for Five Złoty" in 1858.

Preparation of chops

Wash the meat, rub with olive oil, pepper, salt, marjoram, garlic and paprika and set aside in a cool place for several hours. Cut into one centimetre pieces. Tenderise the meat chops with a meat mallet as thinly as is possible. Add the spices and breadcrumbs. First cover with flour, then beaten egg and finally breadcrumbs. Fry chops in hot, but not too high, heat, until they reach a golden colour.

Preparation of cabbage

Put the cabbage into a pot of water. Add the cumin, bay leaf, allspice, and chopped and fried onion. Cook the cabbage until softened. In a frying pan heat the butter, add flour and gradually pour in the broth, stirring well. Heat until the mixture reaches the density of cream. Add the roux to the cabbage, stir and season with salt and pepper.

INGREDIENTS:
Chops:
- *500 grams of boneless pork loin - Olive oil*
- *Flour - Eggs - Breadcrumbs - Salt - Ground pepper - Marjoram - Garlic - Paprika*
Cabbage:
- *500 grams of sauerkraut - 1 onion - Cumin*
- *Allspice - Bay leaf - Ground pepper - Salt*
Roux:
- *2 tablespoons flour - 50 grams butter*
- *100 ml vegetable broth*

50

$\mathcal{R}$IBS IN HONEY
(ŻEBERKA W MIODZIE)

Preparation

Wash meat, and marinate in olive oil and spices. Allow to stand for several hours in a cold place. Fry in hot oil on all sides with honey. Put into a pot with the amount of water with which the meat has been covered. Add chopped onion and garlic and spices. Cover and stew 2 hours. Remove the lid and cook for about 1 hour to reduce the sauce.

INGREDIENTS:

- *1 kilogram of ribs*
- *2 onions*
- *4 cloves of garlic*
- *3 tablespoons of honey*
- *Ground pepper*
- *Bay leaf*
- *Marjoram*
- *Olive oil*
- *Salt*

Poultry

DUCK WITH APPLES
(KACZKA Z JABŁKAMI)

Combines fruit with meat, originating in the Orient. Apples were valued because they were believed to have magical power, guaranteeing health, peace and love.

Preparation

Wash the duck, drain, cut away fat and rub with garlic, salt, orange juice, pepper and marjoram. Allow to stand for several hours in a cold place. Cut apples into eighths. Sew up the duck from the side of the neck and place inside the apple. Insert it into the casserole dish with melted butter on the bottom. On the top spread with butter and sprinkle with water. Bake in a preheated to 200°C oven for 1 hour, covered. From time to time pour onto the duck sauce, and sprinkle with water. In the middle of roasting place next to the duck hollowed apples with cranberries in the middle. Remove the cover from the dish and bake until the duck is tender.

INGREDIENTS:

- 1 duck - eight sour apples - 1 teaspoon marjoram - 3 tablespoons cranberry - Orange juice or blueberries - 2 tablespoons olive oil - Lemon juice - Sugar - Ground pepper - Marjoram - Salt

$\mathcal{F}$ILLED ROAST CHICKEN
(KURCZE PIECZONE Z NADZIENIEM)

Preparation

Wash the chicken, rub with salt and stand for several hours in the refrigerator. Grind liver with soaked and wrung bread roll. Blend the butter and egg yolks. To the butter add liver, peeled and finely chopped almonds and soaked raisins. Add the breadcrumbs and stir. At the end, add, still stirring, whipped egg whites. Season to taste with salt, pepper and chopped parsley. Stuff the chicken and sew up. Put in an oven preheated to 220°C and bake for about 1.5 hours.

INGREDIENTS:

- 1 chicken
- 300 grams of chicken liver
- A Kaiser bread roll (bread roll with a cross pattern on top) - 100 grams of breadcrumbs
- 4 eggs - 250 grams of butter
- 100 grams of raisins - 100 grams of almonds
- 1 parsley - Salt - Ground pepper

LIVER WITH APPLES
(WĄTRÓBKA Z JABŁKAMI)

Preparation

Wash liver and put in a pan with hot oil. Add chopped onion in half-moon slices, pepper and marjoram. Strongly fry the liver. Finally, add sliced apples. Heat briefly and season with salt.

INGREDIENTS:

- 500 grams of chicken liver
- 4 onions
- Oil
- 4 vine-flavoured apples
- Marjoram
- Salt
- Ground pepper

FRIED CARP
(KARP SMAŻONY)

Carp was known in Europe as early as 350 years BC, but the Polish sojourned at the beginning of the thirteenth century, probably from the Tatar onslaught. In later times carp was one of the most important fish reared in ponds, including monasteries. As a Lenten dish is traditionally associated was and still is with Christmas Eve.

Preparation

Scrape and clean the fish, slice, and rub in seasoning. Put in an earthenware pot, layered between slices of onion and leave in a cool place overnight. Coat the carp in flour, beaten egg, spices and breadcrumbs. Fry the fish on both sides with hot oil. Put on the dish with a piece of butter on top. Fry onion rings in the fat and serve with the fish.

INGREDIENTS:

- Carp - 4 large onions
- Bay leaf - Ground pepper
- Allspice - Coriander
- 250 grams of butter
- Wheat flour - 2 eggs
- Breadcrumbs

TROUT IN FOIL
(PSTRĄG W FOLII)

Preparation

Wash trout, dry and rub with salt and pepper. Wash mushrooms and cut into flakes and fry in butter. Carrots are cut into sticks. Cut the onions finely and fry. Everything is mixed with the lemon juice, tarragon and chopped parsley. Place this filling inside the fish and fasten with toothpicks. On the buttered foil sheets lay the fish, wrap the foil tightly and place the dish in a preheated to 220°C oven. Bake fish for 30 minutes.

INGREDIENTS:

Trout:
- 4 trout- 4 sheets of aluminium foil
- 2 tablespoons butter - Basil - 2 carrots
- 1 onion - Ground pepper - Salt
Filling:
- 150 grams of mushrooms - 1 tablespoon of
butter - 1 tablespoon of lemon juice
- Parsley - Dried tarragon

FRIED ZANDER

(SANDACZ SMAŻONY)

Preparation

Scrape the fish, wash and gut. Cut into pieces, season with salt and pepper and set aside in a cool place for about 1 hour. Remove salt from the fish with tissue paper. Dip the pieces of fish in beaten egg, then in breadcrumbs. Heat fat in a frying pan and fry the fish on both sides until the skin is golden brown.

To fish can be served salad or sauerkraut.

INGREDIENTS:

- *1 zander*
- *Egg*
- *Breadcrumbs*
- *Salt*
- *Oil for frying*

Vegetarian dishes

DUMPLINGS WITH PLUMS
(KNEDLE ZE ŚLIWKAMI)

Prepared in the form of balls of dough. Originates from Germany where it is called „Knödl". Dumplings in Germany are stuffed with meat or spinach. The Polish specialty is to stuff them with plums.

Preparation of the dough

Wash potatoes, peel and cook until soft. When rain and cooled grind with the sieved flour, egg and salt. Knead the dough.

Preparation of dumplings

Form the dough into roll with a diameter of 1.5 cm, cut it into pieces and flatten to get round slices. Put inside the chopped fruit and with the dough form a ball. Drop into salted, boiling water and cook until they float to the top. Place on platter, sprinkle with buttered breadcrumbs and sprinkle with sugar. You can also pour cream onto the dumplings.

INGREDIENTS:
Dough:
- 1 kilogram of potatoes - 300 grams of wheat flour - 1 egg - Salt
Filling:
- 500 grams of plums - 40 grams of butter
- Breadcrumbs - Cream - Salt - Sugar

60

KOPYTKA
(DUMPLINGS)

Preparation

Wash potatoes, peel and cook. Knead when they are still warm. Add flour, egg and knead the dough. Form a 1.5 cm roll and cut into pieces 1 cm thick. Drop the dumplings into boiling, salted water and cook until they float to the top. Serve topped with sauce or butter.

INGREDIENTS:

- 1 kilogram of potatoes
- 200 grams of flour
- 1 egg

61

PANCAKES
WITH COTTAGE CHEESE

This dish probably originated in Florence, from where it was brought in the sixteenth century into France by Catherine de Medici, when she married the king of the French. From France they were brought to the Poland in the sixteenth century and were originally made of coarse rye flour. They were often baked on a leaf of cabbage and burdock from whence they derived their present name.

Preparation of dough

Mix milk with sparkling water, egg, flour, cream and a pinch of salt. Set aside for about 10 minutes. Pour into a heated pan with oil a thin layer of the dough. After a while, turn over and fry.

Preparation of filling

To the cheese add mixed egg yolk with sugar, vanilla sugar and raisins. Mix and put a thin layer on the baked pancakes. Wrap this in a roll to form pancakes.

Onto the pancakes you can pour cream and sprinkle with sugar.

Pancakes stuffed with meat or cabbages are called croquettes and can eat with red borsch.

INGREDIENTS:

Dough:
- 250 ml of milk - 50 ml of sparkling water - 1 egg
- 50 grams of flour - 1 tablespoon of cream - Salt
Filling:
- 300 grams of cottage cheese - 1 egg yolk
- 1 portion of vanilla sugar - 20 grams of raisins

IEROGI

This dish probably originated in the Far East, and arrived to Poland from Rus. According to tradition, Dominican bishop, Jacek Odrowąż, who in the thirteenth century founded new monasteries in Rus, brought from Kyiv dumplings, known as pierogi. The name probably comes from the Old-Russian word „pir", meaning to celebrate, because originally pierogi were served only during festivals and celebrations. Each celebration had its own distinct type of pierogi with a different name, appearance and stuffing: „Chicken Coops" – for a wedding, „Knysze" - for mourning, „Kolad-ki" - served during carol singing and „Socznie" - on the occasion of a "Name Day".

Preparation of dough

Sift flour, add salt, egg, lukewarm water and knead the dough. Roll out and cut with a glass circular discs. Put in the stuffing prepared earlier. Join the edges of the dough and crimp to form pierogi. Drop them into boiling water and cook until they float to the surface.

Preparation of filling for Russian Pierogi

Wash potatoes, peel and cook until soft. Still warm knead and add cottage cheese, chopped and fried onion, salt and pepper. Mix and knead.

Preparation of filling for Pierogi with Cabbage

Boil the cabbage with a little water until soft. Drain and cut into fine, add finely chopped and fried onion and also salt and pepper. In a pan fry the cabbage and put it into the pierogi.

Preparation of filling for Pierogi with Cottage Cheese

Mix the cheese with egg yolk, sugar, vanilla sugar and raisins.

Preparation of filling for Pierogi with Meat

Wash the meat and fry on each side. Boil until tender, together with the peeled vegetables. Cool and grind the meat through a meat grinder. Add egg, breadcrumbs, and spices and fry in butter, with finely chopped onion.

INGREDIENTS:

Dough:
- 500 grams of flour - Salt - 1 egg
Filling for Russian Pierogi:
- 1 kilogram of potatoes - Cottage cheese
- 3 onions - Salt - Ground pepper
Pierogi with Cabbage:
- 1 kilogram of sauerkraut - 1 onion - Salt
- Ground pepper
Pierogi with Cheese:
- 500 grams of cottage cheese - 1 egg yolk
- Vanilla sugar - Raisins
Pierogi with Meat:
- 500 grams of pork (ham or shoulder)
- Pack of soup vegetables
- 1 large onion - 1 egg - 3 tablespoons of breadcrumbs - Salt
- Ground pepper - Marjoram

CURD CHEESE DUMPLINGS
(KLUSKI LENIWE)

Preparation

Knead the cheese with flour and egg. Make the dough rollers about 2 cm thick and cut into cubes. Drop into boiling water and cook until float in the surface. Strain and on a plate pour on butter fried with breadcrumbs.

Sprinkle the dumplings with sugar.

INGREDIENTS:

- 500 grams of cottage cheese
- *100 grams of wheat flour*
- *1 egg*
- *Butter*

POTATO PANCAKES
(PLACKI ZIEMNIACZANE)

Potatoes, originating in South America, specifically from the slopes of the Andes, came to Europe on board the ships of Portuguese conquistadors in the early sixteenth century. They were brought into Poland in 1863 from Vienna by King John III Sobieski after he helped to defend the city against the Turks. The potato bush was a gift for Queen Marie. In the beginning they were not popular and were served as food for pigs, but soon, especially in years of crop failure, were used to supplement the diet.

Potato pancakes were created as a substitute for bread. Even a few rotten potatoes were immediately grated and baked, to avoid further deterioration.

Preparation

Wash potatoes, peel and grate, preferably on a dedicated grinder for grating potatoes. You can also grate on an ordinary grater with small holes. Pour off the liquid portion, which rises from the grating of potatoes. Add flour, egg and finely chopped and fried onion. Season with salt, pepper and marjoram to taste. Mix well and fry in hot oil, pouring into the pan with a spoon small pancakes.

Potato pancakes may be served in various ways: with sugar, with cream or the spice „Maggie".

INGREDIENTS:
- 500 grams of potato - 500 grams flour
- 1 egg - 1 onion - Marjoram
- Salt - Ground pepper

RACUCHY

(PANCAKES WIH APPLES)

Food commonly found in people's kitchens, the former often eaten on New Year's Eve and the Shrove Tuesday. In Silesia, sometimes called „dołki", ("holes"), due to the formation of the recess in the middle.

Preparation

Mix flour with egg yolks and curd milk. Add the separated egg whites. Peel an apple, cut into slices and dip in the mixture. Place on a heated pan with fat. Fry pancakes until golden brown.

Serve powdered with ice sugar.

INGREDIENTS:

- *500 grams of flour*
- *2 eggs*
- *300 ml of curd milk*
- *2 tablespoons of sugar*
- *Salt*
- *Oil or lard*
- *1 apple*

YEAST CAKE
(BABKA DROZDZOWA)

Traditional cake associated with Easter. Bake cakes were frequently regarded as a „mystery" amongst women. Cakes were treated with great care in order that they were not dropped. For example, they were laid on a feather-bed.

Preparation

Pound the yeast with sugar and a few spoons of milk. Allow to stand in warm place for 10 minutes. Sift the flour and knead thoroughly with warm milk, eggs, melted but cooled butter, a pinch of salt, aroma of vanilla, and yeast. Put the cake, covered with cotton cloth, in a warm place for 1 hour until it rises. Knead again and place, sprinkle with breadcrumbs and spread with butter into a greased baking tin. Wait until it rises further and later put into a preheated 150°C oven. Bake for about 45 minutes.

INGREDIENTS:
- 500 grams of flour - 150 grams of sugar
- 250 ml milk - 5 egg yolks - 40 grams of yeast
- 100 grams of butter - Vanilla flavour
- Breadcrumbs - Salt

CENCI
(FAWORKI)

Otherwise known as crisp pastry faworki are traditionally associated with Maundy Thursday, the last Thursday before Lent. Starting the last week of the holiday, it was, in the Polish tradition, a special day where you could eat to your heart's content

Preparation

Mix the flour with chopped butter, add egg yolks, sugar, alcohol, sour cream and a pinch of salt. Knead the dough until bubbles appear. Cover with a cloth and set aside in a cool place for 1 hour. Roll out the dough thinly, cut out rectangular pieces of size 3 x 10 cm, make a cut in the middle and put one end through the hole. Create, in this way, the characteristic shape of faworki. Fry the faworki on both sides in hot fat. After frying place the faworki on a paper towel to drain off the fat. Sprinkle with icing sugar.

INGREDIENTS:

- 250 grams of flour - 4 egg yolks - 100 grams of cream - 1 tablespoon of alcohol - Salt - 40 grams of icing sugar

EKS
(FRUITCAKE)

This cake was already known in ancient Rome. It was made out of barley flour with raisins and pine nuts. In the Middle Ages, honey was added to it. Otherwise it may be derived from the German name of „zwieback", providing a dual method of baking the cake. To the baked cake were added delicacies and the cake was baked once again.

Preparation

Blend butter with eggs and a pinch of salt. During the blending add sieved flour in small portions. When a smooth mixture is achieved, drop in soaked raisins and chopped candied fruits, (dipped in flour), and baking powder. Mix thoroughly. Pour the mixture into a greased baking tin and put into a preheated oven. Bake at 200°C for 45 minutes.

INGREDIENTS:

- 250 grams of wheat flour - 250 grams of butter - 100 grams of sugar - 4 eggs - 150 grams of various candied fruit - 100 grams of raisins - 2 teaspoons of baking powder

MAKOWIEC
(POPPY-SEED CAKE)

The dough contains a large amount of poppy seeds, which in folk tradition symbolized fertility. Makowiec was traditionally eaten on Christmas Eve as a method of ensuring happiness. Young girls of the day ate poppy seeds in order to quickly find a husband.

Preparation of the dough

Pound the yeast in warm milk and let stand for several minutes. Add flour, melted but cooled butter, egg yolks, sugar and salt and knead dough. Allow to stand for half an hour in a warm place.

Preparation of poppy seeds

Soak poppy seeds in boiling water, allow them to cool, and grind in a meat grinder three times. Add pre-soaked raisins, finely chopped nuts, honey and sugar. Beat the egg whites and gently stir with mass of poppies.

Preparation of poppy cake

Roll out the dough into thin rectangles, coat with egg whites and cut into pieces. Close the dough with poppy seeds in the roulade and paste at the connection. Set aside for 30 minutes to rise. Put the dough in the oven preheated to 180°C and bake for 45 minutes. Pour icing onto the cooled cake.

INGREDIENTS:
Dough:
- 500 grams of wheat flour - 250 ml lukewarm

milk - 150 grams of butter - 4 egg yolks
- 40 grams of yeast - 6 tablespoons of sugar
- 1.5 tablespoons of oil - Salt - 10 grams of
vanilla sugar
Poppy filling:
- 500 grams of poppy seeds - 250 grams of
sugar - 100 grams of raisins - 50 grams of
alnuts - 50 grams of honey - 50 grams of
butter- One egg white (from the dough)

MAZUREK
(EASTER CAKE)

A cake, probably of Turkish origin, that arrived in Poland in the seventeenth century. Over the course of time it became a traditional cake, baked at Easter. After a long period of Lent, the Easter cake became a reward for the faithful for temperance in eating. For hostesses it was an opportunity to demonstrate their culinary artistry. Historically, Easter cake was made of several kinds of cake sandwiched with marmalade and jam.

Preparation

Mix flour with egg, caster sugar and butter. Knead the dough and let it stand for half an hour in the refrigerator. Roll out the dough thinly into two rectangles of the size of the planned Easter cake. Put one rectangle into a greased baking pan. Divide the second rectangle into three parts, roll them and spread with scrambled egg. Also spread the egg on the first rectangle. Decorate the first rectangle with the folded dough. Put the dough into an oven, preheated to 200° C. After 10 minutes take out, smear with jam and bake for about 20 minutes more. After baking sprinkle with sweetmeats.

INGREDIENTS:

Dough:
- *180 grams of flour*
- *50 grams of caster sugar*
- *50 grams of butter*
- *1 egg*
Garnish:
- *50 grams of icing sugar*
- *1 lemon - 50 grams of jam*
- *candied fruits - sweetmeats*

PĄCZKI
(DOUGHNUTS)

According to tradition, doughnuts are the invention of Mrs. Krapf, who baked them during the siege of Vienna by Turks in 1683. Thus, the Austrian name 'Krapfen'. The tradition of eating doughnuts on Fat Thursday in Poland appeared in the seventeenth century. It was believed that eating even one doughnut on this day would bring success in life. Originally, they were baked with harder dough and stuffed with pork fat, bacon and meat.

Preparation

Melt the yeast in warm milk, add 100 grams of flour, a spoonful of sugar and let it stand for several minutes in a warm place. Melt the butter in a pot and cool it down. Mix eggs with sugar and a pinch of salt and add to the butter. Add butter, milk, alcohol, vanilla and grated orange peel to the well-risen yeast. Knead the dough until bubbles emerge and set aside in a warm place for 30 minutes to rise, covered with cloth. Roll out the well-risen dough 1 cm thick and cut out circles with a glass. Put half a teaspoon of marmalade on them and stick together to form a spherical shape. Pour oil into a pot and heat it until a piece of dough rises quickly and becomes golden brown. Place the doughnuts in the oil and fry them until they float to the surface. Take them out, strain them, and put on a paper towel to remove an excess of oil. Sprinkle with caster sugar.

INGREDIENTS:

- 600 grams of flour - 200 ml of milk - 10 egg yolks
- 1 egg - 1 orange - 100 grams of butter
- 3 tablespoons of sugar - 3 tablespoons of oil - 120 grams of yeast
- 2 tablespoons of alcohol
- 1 vanilla sugar - oil - sugar - salt - rose jam - caster sugar

GINGERBREAD

(PIERNIK)

This name derives from the Old Polish word 'pierny', i.e. peppery. It was a luxury cake with spices obtained mainly from India, which were very expensive in the Middle Ages. Therefore the cake became traditionally associated with the Hanseatic towns, as a symbol of their overseas trade. In Poland Torun was such a city, famous to this day for its gingerbread, which appeared there in the seventeenth century. There are two forms of gingerbread: hard biscuits sandwiched with marmalade, decorated on the top with chocolate, nuts and raisins, and rectangular, soft cakes layered with marmalade.

Preparation

Put the honey, sugar and butter into a pot and heat to the boil, stirring slowly. Cool down the mix and add the flour, eggs, spices, cloves – grinded in a mortar, with alt and baking soda, dissolved in half a glass of milk. Knead the dough well. Divide into three equal parts and roll them out. Bake in preheated oven at 180°C for 20 minutes. Cool down the pieces of dough and spread marmalade. Cover with baking paper and a chopping board, pressing down with something heavy. Lay aside for several days. After it becomes brittle, pour on icing.

INGREDIENTS:

- 500 grams of honey
- 2 glasses of sugar
-250 grams of butter
- 600 grams of wheat flour - 3 eggs
- 3 flat teaspoons of baking soda
- half a cup of milk
- half a teaspoon of salt - cloves
- cinnamon - nutmeg

CHEESECAKE

(SERNIK Z BAKALIAMI)
WITH SWEETMEATS

A luxury cake, in the past baked only during the holidays and weddings, in wealthy households. Once milk was a commercial product which was rarely used in the menu of poorer households.

Preparation

Melt the butter, add egg yolks, baking powder, sugar, vanilla sugar and cream. Add to the sifted flour and knead the dough. Roll out the dough and place on a mould, greased with butter and sprinkled with bread crumbs. Separate the whites from the egg yolks and whip until stiff, adding one tablespoon of caster sugar. Mix egg yolks with sugar and add the cheese, cream and pudding powder. Mix gently slowly adding egg whites. Add sweetmeats, raisins and grated orange peel and mix gently. Put the cheese mass on the dough. Put into the preheated oven and bake for 1.5 h at 140°C.

INGREDIENTS:

Dough:
- 250 grams of flour - 100 grams of butter
- 2 egg yolks - 1 teaspoon of baking powder
- vanilla sugar - 100 grams of sugar
- 3 tablespoons of cream
Cheese:
- 1 kilogram of minced cottage cheese
- 5 eggs - 200 grams of sugar
- pudding powder - raisins - orange peel
- 1 tablespoon of cream
- chocolate glaze - sweetmeats

ZARLOTKA
(APPLE PIE)

Preparation

Knead the dough with all the additives until well mixed and put in a cold place for 30 minutes. Peel and dice the apples. Stew them until tender, with sugar and spices. Divide the dough into two equal parts. Grate one part of the dough on a coarse grater and place on the bottom of a buttered mold. Put stewed apples onto the mold and grate the second part of the dough on the top. Bake until the pastry is golden brown on the top. Serve warm, sprinkled with caster sugar.

INGREDIENTS:

Dough:
- *500 grams of coarse flour*
- *1 box of vegetable butter*
- *0.5 a glass of sugar*
- *3 tablespoons of thick cream*
- *2 flat teaspoons of baking powder*
- *4 eggs*

Filling:
- *2 kilograms of sour apples*
- *a few cloves - caster sugar*
- *1 glass of sugar - cinnamon*

POTATO CAKE

(BABKA ZIEMNIACZANA)

The dish was created in the nineteenth century; traditionally associated with Podlasie and Suwalki regions.

Preparation

Peel and grate the potatoes and let them stand for 15 minutes. Collect the potato juice. Add eggs, pepper, salt, marjoram and finely chopped and stir-fried smoked bacon and onion. Stir everything together and put into greased baking mould. Bake in the oven at 200°C for 1.5 hours.

INGREDIENTS:

- 2 kilograms of potatoes
- 2 eggs - 200 grams of smoked bacon
- 400 grams of flour - 1 onion
- marjoram - salt - ground pepper

KARTACZE
(GRAPE-SHOTS)

The dish traditionally associated with Podlasie and Lithuanian culinary tradition in Poland – 'ceppelins' of Sejny. It was originally served as a soup made from cooked meat, with smoked bacon and herbs.

Preparation

Peel and grate 1 kilogram of potatoes and wrap in a linen cloth. Tightly squeeze the juice into a glass. After 10 minutes, pour off the water from the top, leaving only the starch. Cook the remaining 300 grams of potatoes, put through a meat grinder. To the grinded potatoes add cooked potatoes, potato flour, squeezed potato starch, egg and salt. Stir and knead everything until well mixed. Mince the meat and add the finely chopped and stir-fried onion, garlic, marjoram, pepper and salt. Mix carefully and knead. Put a little potato dough on the hand and create a pie. In the middle of the pie put a prepared meat ball. Wrap the dough and stick it so that the whole meat is inside. Shape in the form of eggs or 'zeppelins'. Boil a pot of salted water and add a tablespoon of oil. Put in as many grape-shots as can fit in one layer. After 2 minutes, loosen them with a wooden spoon from the bottom and turn them over. Cook them for about 40

minutes on low heat. Take out the grape-shots from the water and serve with finely chopped, stir-fried onion and bacon.

INGREDIENTS:
- 1.3 kilograms of potatoes - 500 gram of pork
- 2 tablespoons of potato flour - 1 egg - 1 onion
- 100 grams of bacon

KULEBIAK

A traditional dish of Podlasie regional cuisine. It originated in Slavic areas. The name, however, comes from the German word 'Kohlgeback' which meant dough stuffed with cabbage. The recipe with a whole egg inside comes from Russia.

Preparation

Cook the chopped cabbage and strain. Finely chop the onion and mushrooms and stir-fry. Mix the whole and season with salt and pepper. Ingredients for the dough mix carefully and knead. Put aside, covered with cloth, in a warm place. After half an hour knead the dough once more. Roll it out into a flat pie. Place the filling on the pie and roll it in, joining both ends. Leave the pie to rise. Bake for about 1 hour at 180°C.

In various parts of Poland different recipes are used. Sauerkraut is often added instead of cabbage.

INGREDIENTS:
Dough:
- 300 grams of flour - 150 grams of butter
- 3 egg yolks - 250 ml of milk - 40 grams of yeast - salt - sugar
Filling:
- 250 grams of cabbage - 2 onions - oil
- 50 grams of dried mushrooms

PYR WITH GZIK

A traditional dish originating from Greater Poland. 'Pyry' in the dialect of Greater Poland mean potatoes, and 'gzik' – cottage cheese with chives.

Preparation

Scrub potatoes and wrap in aluminium foil. Put into a preheated oven and bake for 20 minutes at temperature of 180° C. We can do it also in a bonfire or fireplace. Grind the cheese and add finely chopped: onion, radish, garlic, parsley, chives and hard-boiled egg. Pour cream and mix everything. Remove potatoes from the aluminium foil and cut in half. Spread a little butter and place on a large spoonful of the cheese.

INGREDIENTS:
- 10 potatoes
- 300 ml of cream (18% of fat)
- 500 grams of cottage cheese
- 1 egg - 1 onion - a few radishes
- dill - 2 cloves of garlic - parsley
- a bunch of chives - butter - salt
- ground pepper

*W*ERESZCZAKI

A traditional dish of Masurian cuisine.

Preparation

Cut pork fat into strips, and the pork into thick cubes, salt and stir-fry in a pan. Put the meat into a pot with beetroot acid. Add pepper, allspice, and cook covered until tender. At the end of cooking, add the grated bread and cook without cover briefly until the dish thickens.

Serve with cooked potatoes or grits.

INGREDIENTS:

- *500 grams of pork loin*
- *100 grams of pork fat*
- *0.5 liter of beetroot acid*
- *50 grams of grated bread*
- *ground pepper*
- *salt*
- *allspice*
- *marjoram*

Preserves

MARINATED MUSHROOMS
(GRZYBY MARYNOWANE)

For centuries, the immensity of the Polish forests guaranteed the abundance of mushrooms that have been used for many meals. Marinating, i.e. storage in vinegar, was a way of food preservation. The most often marinated mushrooms are: saffron milk cap, boletus, xerocomus, armillaria mellea, golden chanterelle and suillus.

Preparation

Wash the mushrooms and cook in salted water with onion for about 30 minutes, until tender. Dissolve the vinegar in the boiled water at a ratio of 1:3. Add a pinch of sugar, pepper, allspice and bay leaf. You can add small onions to the pickle. Pour over the mushrooms, previously placed in the jar.

INGREDIENTS:
- 750 ml of water - 250 ml of 10% vinegar
- 3 teaspoons of sugar - 1.5 teaspoon of salt
- ground pepper - allspice - bay leaves
- 1 onion

SAUERKRAUT

(KAPUSTA KISZONA)

Pickling is a natural method to preserve some foods, especially vegetables such as cucumber, cabbage, garlic, onions, beets, green beans, peppers, cauliflower, mushrooms and apples. In the process of pickling, caused by lactic acid bacteria, lactic fermentation occurs that stops rotting and produces lactic acid and, in small amounts, acetic acid and alcohol. Pickled products are nutritionally very valuable because they contain large amounts of vitamin C and mineral salts.

Preparation

Chop or finely grate the cabbage. Wash the container for pickling. This can be a plastic or wooden barrel or a stone vessel. Place on the bottom 5 cm layer of cabbage, sprinkle it with salt, and then pestle it to get the juice. Pour fine grated carrot and a little sugar on the top. Put another layer of cabbage and act like with the first one, until the container is filled. Place the keg in a warm place for 3 days and cover it with a linen cloth. Then move the barrel in a cool place, cover the cabbage with a plate and press with something heavy. After two days make a few holes in the cabbage with a long, thin stick. Repeat this operation every 4 days, until the gas ceases to be emitted (about 3 weeks). After 1 month, put the sauerkraut into glass jars, well-compress it and twist the jars. If you want less pickled cabbage you need to stop the fermentation process earlier and pasteurize the jars.

INGREDIENTS:

- *cabbage*
- *carrots*
- *salt*

PICKLED CUCUMBERS
(OGÓRKI KISZONE)

Pickling of cucumbers was known in Eastern Europe for centuries. Cucumbers pickled for a few days are called low-salt cucumbers and known as pickled cucumbers later on. Small pickled and later marinated cucumbers are called gherkins.

Preparation

Wash the cucumbers and put them for 15 minutes in water. Boil the water and cool it down so it is not hot. Add salt to the cooled water and mix thoroughly. Take the cucumbers out from the water and put them into a jar, add a piece of horseradish root, 2 cloves of garlic, a large stalk of dill and mustard grains. Twist the jar lid thoroughly.

INGREDIENTS:

- *a few cucumbers for pickling*
- *30 g of salt per 1 liter of water*
- *a piece of horseradish root*
- *2 cloves of garlic*
- *1 large dill*
- *20 grains of mustard*

Photography by: Jolanta and Rafał Jabłoński

Text by Rafał Jabłoński

Graphic design by: Rafał and Paweł Jabłoński

Print: Perfekt, Warsaw

ISBN 978-83-65489-15-9

FESTINA Publishers, tel/fax +48 (22) 842-54-53, cellphone: +48 602 324 409
e-mail: wydawnictwo@festina.org.pl, www.festina.org.pl

WARSAW